Simple Intelligence

G.O. (Get Optimistic)

How acronyms and affirmations can truly work to your advantage

PIERRE CAMPBELL

Copyright Information

Print: ISBN 978-0-959792-0-1
Epub: ISBN 978-0-959792-1-8
Kindle: ISBN 978-0-959792-2-5
PDF: ISBN 978-0-959792-3-2

Simple Intelligence™. Copyright © 2012 Published by The Leadership Network Inc., Loudoun, VA. All rights reserved, including the right of reproduction in whole or in parts in any form without the written permission. http://www.pierrecamp.com/

Simple Intelligence™
Registered trademark of PierreCamp, LLC & The Leadership Network Inc., Herndon, VA

All rights reserved, no part of this book may be reproduced in whole or in parts in any form without the written permission of the author except in the case of brief quotations embodied in critical articles and review.

Cover photo by Brandon Bryant

Cover and interior book design by Laura Carter
www.carterpublishingstudio.com

Graphic design of PierreCamp and Leadership Network materials by Jerome McLain
www.maxmediastudios.com

Website by Matthew Jackson

What leaders are saying about *Simple Intelligence:*

"A couple of years ago, I had a medical emergency that reminded me of living each day to the fullest, because you never know what tomorrow will bring. Pierre Campbell's *Simple Intelligence* has that underlying message—to live and love as if tomorrow might not come. I appreciate Pierre for his *Simple Intelligence*. My favorite acronym has to be "WOMAN" because the most influential people in my life have been women."

Dr. Miguel Corona
www.MiguelCorona.com

"This is a wise and deep-hearted book, a must-read in today's world. It has something to be learned by people from all walks of life. Change your life by reading this book and practicing the exercises."

Dr. Michael Otaigbe
Campus Dean
Strayer University

"Pierre is off to a great start with a presentation of ideas that will serve you well. The use of acronyms makes complex life skills easily and readily accessible to those of us crushed by the tempo of the daily grind. I particularly liked the reminder to be a mentor at every opportunity. *Simple Intelligence* is a great platform that we will hear much more of."

Dr. Bob Nolley
Campus Dean
Strayer University

"Mr. Campbell is truly a dynamic leader. His strategic, creative, and tactical execution of various initiatives to enhance personal image, academic excellence, and self productivity are legendary. He has a depth of knowledge in terms of one's own psychology that positively affects many individuals' life experiences and personal growth. He has valuable experience in encouraging young executives, students, athletes, and others, converting them to focused scholars with winning spirits. He possesses a unique insight that can enhance one's personal cognitive experience. He has executed successful self-improvement programs that improve personal efficiencies and self-esteem. Personal growth and exhibited best-in-class performance result from his training style and techniques. He is a decisive professional life coach who responds to challenges with confidence, determination, sincere concern and focus on the individuals whom he has served as mentor. Mr. Campbell has exhibited a generous commitment to community service by virtue of his personal example and strong family ties. I recommend Mr. Pierre Campbell's book with the highest regard."

PEDRO BARRY
Project Manager

"Pierre's discovery that LOVE and GRACE are ALWAYS present in the midst of tragedy and life's difficulties is priceless, empowering and inspirational. It is a powerful and timely message in a world that has lost hope. That discovery, coupled with his articulation of the TRUTH that everyone has a purpose and many gifts which lead them to their purpose in life, will plant the seed of HOPE that will bless individuals, families, communities, nations and the world."

MEADE MALONE
Best selling Author, *Unbreakable Spirit—Rising Above the Impossible and The Plan—Unlocking God's Financial Blessing for your Life*
www.MeadeMalone.com

"Pierre Campbell walks us through the importance of changing the way we look at everyday words. Through his book *Simple Intelligence,* he helps us discover the positive in the negative. It is only as we begin to look at our words differently that we will change the way we think, thereby changing our outcomes. Pierre Campbell is a dynamic motivational speaker who gives us the opportunity to take home some of the acronyms that have influenced his speaking engagements. I would recommend this book as a way to discover the power of words."

LYNN CONTEH, CEO
Perteh

"Internationally known motivational speaker Pierre Campbell puts his thoughts into writing in *Simple Intelligence*. Pierre is very open, and shares personal trials that have shaped his life and how he has learned to see positive even in the negative. I recommend this book to help individuals have a positive outlook through acronyms. *Simple Intelligence* is a resource to have in hand both in the office and at home. This book can be referred to on a regular basis to help change how we look at situations in life. His creativity in words is refreshing and resourceful."

ABDUL CONTEH
Sierra Leone, Africa

"Some say that "common sense" is no longer common. Pierre Campbell's *Simple Intelligence* is a refreshing collection of simple strategies. Once applied to your daily life you will exponentially increase your status, mindset, relationships, and intelligence."

RAE MAJORS-WILDMAN, CEO, FOUNDER
www.AllTheWaySuccess.com

"Pierre Campbell is a dynamic young man who will help you to live your life with power and purpose. In this book, he gives you creative ideas that will empower you and push you to do more, be more, and achieve more! Read it and share it with friends and family who need a word of encouragement in their lives! And make a point to keep your eye on Pierre...he is a young man who is going places!!!!"

WILLIE JOLLEY
Best-Selling Author of *A Setback Is A Setup For A Comeback & An Attitude of Excellence!*
www.WillieJolley.com

Dedication

First and foremost, this book is dedicated
to my Lord and Savior Jesus Christ.
I would not have been able to create this
if it were not for His grace and mercy.

≈

Table of Contents

Foreword by Darrell "Coach D" Andrews ix

Acknowledgements xi

A Message to You and My Unborn Children 1

Introduction 3

Putting life into Perspective 5

Inspiration 7

Explanation 9

Positive Thought Process 11

Acronyms and Affirmations 13

Mission 37

References 38

Foreword

IN CLOSE TO TWO DECADES of inspiring the lives of millions of people as a speaker and author, I have learned many valuable things regarding developing human potential. A few of the most valuable truths I have embraced are the following:

- All people were born with a gift from God that they can use to impact the planet in a positive way.

- It is impossible to achieve a dream on your own.

- Some people do more with their lives in a week than most do in a year.

- Attitude is not everything. Attitude plus aptitude is everything.

- A powerful vision will take an average person and make them legendary.

- And lastly—*People in the pursuit of their purpose have a tendency to overcomplicate things. In doing so, their lives become so complex that dreams often remain only dreams.*

What Pierre Campbell is proposing in his book *Simple Intelligence* is that our life endeavors do not have to be overly complicated. If we internalize simple wisdom habitually, we can program our minds to take the steps necessary to accomplish our life and career goals.

I liken this revelation to an athlete in training. Years ago, when I played college football, it seemed to me that we went through pretty much the same routine day after day after day. We would practice our plays, run hills, hit each other in scrimmages time and time again. I would then go to the weight room and lift weights day after day after day. What drove us young men to give up part of our summers to spend day after day in pads weighing up to 30 pounds, in 80+ degrees temperatures to prepare for game days on the gridiron? It was the vision of one day winning our conference championship, and going as far as we could in the playoffs. This was the bigger vision for our team. The big vision was the motivator, but the daily routine was the preparation. What we did daily in practice and in the weight room was preparation for our vision of winning the championship. Mike Murdock puts it this way: *Your future success is hidden in your daily routine.* As Pierre Campbell says it, it is *Simple Intelligence.*

In reading this book, I believe that you will be well on your way to establishing habits in your thinking that will help you in your pursuit of personal excellence. If you develop your *Simple Intelligence*, you will begin to understand and maximize your potential in a new and exciting way.

Darrell "Coach D" Andrews, CSP
Certified Speaking Professional
Author of *How To Find Your Passion And Make A Living At It*
www.coachdspeaks.com

Acknowledgements

PLEASE ENJOY AND SHARE my first thought-provoking personal development book, *Simple Intelligence™*. To my lovely wife, Kim, the love of my life; you and I make one. Thank you for being you. Always know that you are good enough for me just the way you are. I love you. To my mother, Ione, this book is an example of how you've inspired me. I can hear you now in that Jamaican accent "Nothing beat a try but a failure." Here's my try, Mom. To my big brother, Alex, you are an amazing brother, father and friend. Thanks for looking out for me and for bringing my "mini me," nephew Matisse, into the world. To my cousin, Karyl, thank you for assisting me with the formatting process of this book. To my wonderful grandmother, Motherdear, I can hear you singing our song now—"My grandson promise to give me something ting ting ting and the birds them sing." This one's for you, Motherdear.

To the Don Crew from Cheyney University, we are a team for life. Oz, Dorian, Larry, Nate, Kamen, Ibrahim, Abdul, Gary, and the other Dons: always know that Pep has your back. To all my other friends, ex-teammates, and colleagues, I thank you from the bottom of my heart. Whether you believe it or not, you have touched my life. I'm happy to have known you. Special 'Big Ups' to my advisor and producer, Chris Greene, who helped me with the creative process. I would also like to thank my editor, Vicki Lipski, for doing an outstanding job. There are so many other family members and friends whom I have left out. Please know that I love you all and appreciate your support. If you think you have had some kind of positive or negative influence in my life, I love you, too.

A Message to You and My Unborn Children

One of my greatest investments has been my audio library. Use a highlighter and study this book, along with the other books in our library, and you will learn some of the valuable lessons I learned.

- Wait and think before you respond.
- Remember: your response is your responsibility.
- Believe in yourself, put your trust in the Lord, and enjoy your life.
- You only have one chance to live on this earth.
- Learning through your own experience is good. Learning from other people's experiences will help you accomplish your goals much faster.

One of our greatest leaders, Oprah, once said, "Everything passes in its time. It doesn't matter how much money you have, how much power you have, how high you sit on the *Forbes* list, how many times you make the Most Influential list—all of that changes. All of that changes. But what is real, what is lasting, is who you are and what you were meant to bring. What is the gift you were meant to give? And nobody can take that away from you."

- Seek wisdom, knowledge, and understanding, and you will find them.
- Whatever you focus on, you will attract.
- Dream big, visualize your dreams, and have fun.
- Expect the best because you deserve it.
- Accept people for who they are and things for what they are.
- Renew your mind.

One of my mentors, Marcus Buckingham, said, "Build on your strengths and manage around your weaknesses." Always remember to be grateful. Your talents and strengths are important, but your attitude and your ability to get along with people will be the qualities that propel you forward in life. Daddy loves you.

- You're going to have problems, but they are just problems.
- You are a problem solver; take time to think, and you will solve your problems.
- Be a mentor and have a mentor at all times.
- You don't have to know the person personally for them to be your mentor.

Study their books and the stories of their lives; you will learn how to deal with your challenges through their experiences.

The master of personal development, Jim Rohn, once said, "Personal development will make you more valuable to the marketplace." He's also known for saying, "Work harder on yourself than you do on the job." Jim is absolutely correct.

Introduction

EVER SINCE THE BEGINNING OF TIME, people have been searching for the secret to success and positivity. Ultimately, we all have a choice in life. We can think positively or negatively about our circumstances. Choose wisely.

In my travels, I've asked many people: What are the keys to success? Why are some people more successful than others? What's the secret to happiness? Their answers are always interesting, but I've come to a conclusion and narrowed it down to three things.

- Relationships are what matter the most.
- Maintain a positive attitude everyday.
- Personal development lasts a lifetime.

Maintaining a positive attitude can be a very challenging thing to do. The longer we live, the more problems we encounter. Building a strong, faith-filled foundation, and developing mental toughness are what Simple Intelligence™ is designed to do. Thinking positive thoughts has always kept love in my heart; Love is the ultimate form of gratitude. I've learned when you give love you may not receive it from the person you give it to, but love is a very powerful energy that will always come back to you.

Simple Intelligence™ is my philosophy that has helped me to build strong, lasting relationships and puts things in perspective. It turns negative thoughts into positive ones and I end up attracting the right people.

I consider myself a learner, and at the same time, a teacher. In order to fulfill those roles, I decided it would be a good idea to pour some of my knowledge into the lives of others. My friends, family members, and co-workers have wanted me to write a book for many years. One day,

I looked around my apartment at my library of personal development, leadership and management books, and got fed up. That day I asked myself, "What am I doing? I've purchased all these books to study and learn what the great thinkers of the past and present have to teach." It was then; I realized I had something to share as well. This "aha" moment provided the motivation to finally start writing. Sometimes, that's all it takes. These things came to mind at first:

- By learning to LOVE and share, you will live up to your full potential.

- Believe in yourself and become a better friend.

- You need people and we need you.

- We're all connected and once we realize that, we become better people.

- Never compare yourself to others; just ask yourself, what have I done to bring myself closer to my goals and purpose everyday?

- Even the smallest steps in the right direction count in life.

There are times when I sit back and think about decisions I've made, and somehow they all seem to have brought me closer to my most dominant thoughts. They are always positive and optimistic. Like Henry Ford once said, "Whether you think you can or you think you can't—you're right."

As a teacher, I believe Simple Intelligence™ is a learner's dream; it is personal development that will change the speed at which you learn, and increase your curiosity about education. I hope you recommend this book to your family, friends and co-workers. We can start a new positive-thinking revolution with people who exercise what I like to call *Simple Intelligence™*.

Putting Life into Perspective

LIFE IS AN AMAZING JOURNEY, and a gift, for that matter. One of the things about life that no one can debate is that we have one chance to live. We all die, so let us enjoy life while we can. Do all you can do now, love everyone, and leave the hatred behind.

Have you ever felt caught up in your life or work, and then something happened that put things in perspective? I can remember three very important days that really put life in perspective for me. The first day was in the summer of 1994, right before I was scheduled to go away to college. I was at a party, and a friend of mine wanted to give me and some other friends a ride home. My friend was arguing with a girl, who got so mad, she hit my friend's car with a bat. Immediately afterward, a car drove by and let two shots off in the air to break up the fight. I pushed my friend into the car, and jumped in the back seat. It was about 1am, and the windows of the car had very dark tint. We could not see that someone had walked up to the side of the car. A gun went off—my friend had been shot in his face. The gunman ran, and I started to talk to my friend. The amazing part of this story is that my friend was coherent, and he thought he got hit with the bat. I talked him through putting the car in drive, and stepping on the gas so we could get out of there. Everything happened quickly, but at the time it seemed like slow motion. I looked through the back window and saw someone running and shouting at the car. I encouraged my wounded friend and directed him to drive home, which was about three miles away.

The next day, when I went to the police station, the cops told me there was a bullet stuck in the back seat. Whoever might have been lying across the back seat would've been paralyzed, if the bullet had gone through them. That person would have been me and I believe the only reason that bullet did not go through the seat and my friend didn't die was the grace of God.

Then there was the day my mom almost passed away in my arms. She was sick at home with acute asthma. A nurse was there, but the nurse was nervous because she could not find a good vein to inject medicine into my mom's arm. The only thing that saved my mom on that day was God's grace. When she got better, she told me she could hear my voice, but it sounded terribly far away. I was encouraging my mom, telling her that everything would be ok. I'm so glad I was there for her.

Do these two numbers ring a bell for you: 9-11? They ring very loudly for me. You see, I'm a New Yorker who was born in Brooklyn, and raised in Queens. On 9-11, I watched my city go through something movie makers spend millions of dollars to create for people's entertainment. The pictures and videos on the news were, however, far from entertaining on that day. Needless to say, 9-11 was one of the days that put my life in perspective. I will never forget how I felt as I watched the enormous buildings that I used to tour on field trips go down like sand castles being washed away by the ocean. None of the people in those towers, or their families, knew 9-11 would be their last day. I prayed that God's grace would comfort their families, along with the survivors who were trapped underneath the rubble.

In my opinion, the City of New York and our country made it through the disaster because we came together. On that day, and for many days after, people were all the same: we were all Americans. Citizens from all over the country worked together to help rebuild the city. The human race seemed to be the only race then.

The three aforementioned days were definitely game changers for me. The one common theme that I can remember about all those days is that love was in my heart and the grace of God was apparent. I thank God that it always seems to be that way for me. Although those were sad times, they sparked a passion in me and propelled me forward.

I wanted to share those stories with you for two reasons. One is to establish a connection between us, and the other is to show you that no matter how negative a circumstance or situation may seem at the time, there is always a positive way to look at it.

Inspiration

HERE ARE TWO DISTINCT TIMES that have inspired me. The first was the 2007 Super Bowl. This was the first time in the history of the National Football League that a black head coach was guaranteed to win. Lovie Smith was the coach of the Chicago Bears, and Tony Dungy coached the Indianapolis Colts. For many years, black people have played and coached in the NFL, but a black head coach had never won a Super Bowl. That day was an inspiration to many people—fans, players and coaches—because Tony Dungy became our first black head coach to win a Super Bowl. For football fans everywhere, that was a great day in American history.

November 4, 2008 was the day America truly changed. This was the day America elected our first black President, Barack Obama. He is and will always be the proof that people can change. The slogan of his campaign, "Yes we can!" still echoes. This is the type of hope I want to create with my Simple Intelligence™ philosophy. The wonderful thing about people is that we're different colors; and we have different stories, but we're all human beings in God's eyes.

I have an extreme passion for love, leadership, personal development, and human relations. My hope is to encourage you to think about the words you use in a positive way, even if the words are negative.

Everyone on earth has a purpose, and many gifts. I believe our job is to develop our gifts, and then share them with each other; in order to make this world a better place. The key to our wealth and happiness lies in our gifts, which lead us to our purpose in life. Fulfilling my life's mission, which you will find in the last chapter, is one of the most important things to me, simply because my mission keeps me on track with my purpose. It keeps the light in my heart lit, so others can see that there is hope.

Take a really good look at yourself, right now, in your mind's eye or in a mirror. You were wonderfully made; there is no one in the world like you. There was no one exactly like you in the past and there will never be anyone exactly like you in the future. Here's my gift to you: know yourself! Love yourself just the way you are. Continue to learn, because things are constantly changing. If you don't change, you will be forced to, and, quite frankly, being forced to do something sucks. We are all perfect in our own way, and we're worth more than other people's opinions. Even our enemies have something to teach us. Learn the lessons and move on. By faith God has our steps ordered, as long as we believe.

My intention is to share my love with you. I've learned not to push my views on others. That was a very valuable lesson for me, because I've always been known as a motivator. I can help those who want to be helped. I'm having fun writing this book, and I intend to keep writing and sharing my philosophy.

Explanation

WHAT THIS BOOK IS NOT, is a guarantee of your success. I've learned that reading books is essential to our development and growth; however, the art of studying books is even more valuable. This book is not as simple as the title makes it sound. It's actually a little complex; my intention is for you to use the acronyms and affirmations to create a positive outlook.

After reading this book, you will find new ways to use words you thought you knew and understood. I encourage you to study the art of Simple Intelligence™. Formulating each acronym was an absolutely invigorating process for me. The concept of Simple Intelligence™ is to create ***HOPE*** by encouraging you to think positively during tough times; it may even save lives. It will stretch your mind to new levels of awareness and understanding, and it will enhance your vocabulary skills. Simple Intelligence™ is exactly what I needed, and I'm sharing it with you because that's what love is all about.

In school, we learn curriculums filled with mandatory subjects that are not focused on what I believe are the most important things we have to learn in life: social skills. Our education system and media outlets are great, but I believe we need something else. Social skills are important because we deal with people every day of our lives, and our ability to deal with people will take us far in life. The media has us constantly focused on the negative things in our society. Fortunately, you do not have to be in school to learn Simple Intelligence™.

Positive Thought Process

SIMPLE *INTELLIGENCE*™ IS MY PHILOSOPHY of creating a positive thought process through the study of meaningful acronyms. The acronyms, however, are just one facet of my approach to positive thinking. Thinking positively takes practice, but it's definitely worth your happiness and development. How does someone practice positive thinking? Self-talk and prayers have helped me get through the toughest times in my life. Here are four quick and easy tips that you can practice to instantly increase your positive thought process:

1. Gratitude—We always have something to be grateful for, all we have to do is stop and think about where we were in the past. Start using the acronyms to shift your thoughts to gratitude when negative things happen to you, i.e. ***today***: "**T**he **O**nly **D**ay **A**ctually **Y**ours," and ***be***: "**B**reathe **E**asy."

2. Positive self-talk—Begin by claiming all good things over your life with I statements:
   — I can do it. You can do it, "*your name*."
   — I am a winner.
   — I am happy.
   — I am grateful. I love myself.

   Use acronyms such as ***go***: "**G**et **O**ptimistic" for the self-talk process.

   The acronym ***if***: "**I**nduced **F**ailure" will stop you from doubting yourself, if you use the word in a way where it prevents you from moving forward.

3. Smiling—Start smiling at everyone you see and you will feel the remarkable transformation in your spirit. You will also give the gift of happiness to others every time you get a smile in return. ***Reap***: "**R**eward **E**xperienced **A**fter **P**roduction," and ***Luck***: "**L**earning **U**ltimately **C**reates **K**nowledge."

4. Love—I believe love is the most powerful action we can take to shift our thoughts to positivity. ***Love***: "**L**ife's **O**bedient **V**oice **E**ternally."

When you practice the Simple Intelligence™ thought process, you will start to feel good about yourself. Whenever doubt enters your mind, use the acronyms to shift your thoughts to positivity. "Doubt your doubts," is one of my favorite quotes. My acronym for ***doubts*** is "**D**estroying **O**ur **U**seful **B**eliefs **T**hrough **S**abotage."

Remember: everyone has an opinion. You need to develop a strong foundation so you don't get your feelings hurt when someone disagrees with yours. Mental toughness is essential in order to survive in this world. My faith is my strong foundation. Opinions are great and everyone is entitled to their own. Over the years, I've learned how to hold myself accountable for the ways I respond to people's opinions. By taking responsibility for my responses, I am sure to respond in a positive way so my remarks are received in a welcoming fashion.

If you are a person who already uses positive words, great, this book is for you. If you are a person who uses negative words, excellent, this book is for you as well. When you are studying the negative words in this book, you will notice that the affirmations describe a negative action. Each acronym is accompanied by a positive affirmation. The affirmations can help you remember the words. If you are just curious to see how acronyms and affirmations can truly work to your advantage, keep reading. Then study this book. If you do not care, fine, you have read far enough to be positively influenced, and that was my objective. Maybe you can just take a look at a couple of acronyms to see if they're worth your time.

Acronyms & Affirmations

G.O.
Get Optimistic

DAY 1

W.O.R.D

Worth Optimum Results Developed

≈

DAY 2

L.I.F.E

Lucrative Individual Fertile Experience

≈

DAY 3

L.O.V.E

Life's Obedient Voice Eternally

DAY 4

M.A.N

Mature Achiever Naturally

≈

DAY 5

W.O.M.A.N

Winners Offering Magnificent Achievements Needed

"Even the smallest steps count in life."

DAY 6

H.O.P.E

Humans Optimistically Planning Everything

≈

DAY 7

F.A.I.T.H

Foundational Acceptance In The Heart

DAY 8

F.E.A.R

Future Effective Actions Rejected

~

DAY 9

S.T.U.D.Y

Signifies The Universe Developing You

~

DAY 10

T.I.M.E

Temporary Intelligence Man Experiences

> *"Whenever doubt enters your mind, use the acronyms to shift your thoughts to positivity."*

DAY 11

C.H.O.I.C.E

Consistently Having Options In Creative Experiences

DAY 12

L.E.A.D

Love Establishes A Direction

≈

DAY 13

G.O

Get Optimistic

≈

DAY 14

T.O

Transforming Optimistically

DAY 15

A.N.D

Another **N**ecessary **D**ecision

"It keeps the light in my heart lit."

DAY 16

M.I.N.D

Memory **I**mplanted **N**aturally **D**eveloped

≈

DAY 17

B.A.D

Big **A**chievements **D**enied

≈

DAY 18

P.O.S.I.T.I.V.E

Powerful **O**ptimistic **S**uggestions **I**nfluencing **T**hings to **I**ncrease **V**isionary **E**xcellence

DAY 19

R.E.A.P

Reward Experienced After Production

"Know yourself!"

≈

DAY 20

T.O.D.A.Y

The Only Day Actually Yours

≈

DAY 21

A

Acceptance

≈

DAY 22

F.O.R

Fundamentally Overcoming Rage

DAY 23

C.O.M.E

Calling Out Moves Everything

≈

DAY 24

G.R.A.T.I.T.U.D.E

Giving Real Acknowledgments To Initiate Thankfulness
Understanding Decisions Experienced

> *"We always have something to be grateful for; all we have to do is stop and think about where we were in the past."*

DAY 25

P.O.W.E.R

Persistence On Worthy Exercises Revealed

≈

DAY 26

L.U.C.K

Learning Ultimately Creates Knowledge

DAY 27

F.A.T.H.E.R

Future Adviser Teaching Human Ethics Righteously

≈

DAY 28

M.O.T.H.E.R

Mentor Over The House Eternally Respected

≈

DAY 29

S.T.A.R.T

Stimulating The Actions Receiving Truth

DAY 30

G.O.A.L.S

Gathering Of All Learned Studies

≈

DAY 31

T.H.I.N.K

Thoughts Harboring Impressionable Notes Kept

"Love is a very powerful energy that will always come back to you."

DAY 32

U.S.E

Utilize Someone Else

≈

DAY 33

T.H.E

To Have Excellence

> *"Thinking positively takes practice, but it's definitely worth your happiness and development."*

DAY 34

A.I.R

Apparently Is Reality

≈

DAY 35

O.N

Operating Now

≈

DAY 36

E.A.T

Energizing All Things

≈

DAY 37

W.I.S.E

Wisdom Introduces Support Eternally

DAY 38

W.H.O

Winners Have Options

~

DAY 39

P.L.A.N

Provides Longevity And Navigation

*"Treat others the way
they want to be treated."*

DAY 40

V.I.S.I.O.N

Visual Insights Strategizing Intentional Outcomes Needed

~

DAY 41

S.I.N

Stopping Increase Naturally

DAY 42

E.M.P.O.W.E.R

Encouraging Many People On Winning Experiencing Reality

≈

DAY 43

G.R.A.C.E

Goodness Received Accordingly Catapulting Everything

≈

DAY 44

A.C.T

Action Changes Thoughts

DAY 45

I.F

Induced Failure

"Breathe easy today is your day."

DAY 46

F.A.I.L

Fully Attempting Important Lessons

≈

DAY 47

O.N.E

Oldest Number Established

≈

DAY 48

D.O.U.B.T.S

Destroying Our Ultimate Beliefs Through Sabotage

DAY 49

I.T

Initial Transformation

> *"Thinking positively takes practice, but it's definitely worth your happiness and development."*

DAY 50

H.A.T.E

Hoping And Teaching Envy

≈

DAY 51

I.S

Individual Success

≈

DAY 52

V.O.I.C.E

Value Our Inner Core Energy

DAY 53

D.O

Deliver **O**bediently

~

DAY 54

W.A.R

Weak **A**ttitudes **R**evealed

~

DAY 55

I

Individual

"I believe love is the most powerful action we can take to shift our thoughts to positivity."

DAY 56

J.O.Y

Jubilation **O**ver **Y**ou

DAY 57

L.O.S.E

Lasting Only Seconds Emotionally

≈

DAY 58

E.G.O

External Gesture Overused

≈

DAY 59

D.E.A.T.H

Destination Ending A Tired Heart

"If you are a person who already uses positive words, great, this book is for you. If you are a person who uses negative words, excellent, this book is for you as well."

DAY 60

T.R.U.S.T

The Requirement Ultimately Sustained over Time

≈

DAY 61

L.I.V.E

Life's Individual Vision, Eternally

≈

DAY 62

T.R.U.T.H

To Reach Understanding Teaching Humans

DAY 63

I.N.S.P.I.R.A.T.I.O.N

Internal Need Serving People In Renewing Actions
To Introduce Options Naturally

DAY 64

B.E

Breathe Easy

> *"Never compare yourself to others;
> just ask yourself, what have I done to
> bring myself closer to my goals
> and purpose everyday?"*

DAY 65

S.T.R.E.S.S

Stops Talent Reducing Extra Strength Suddenly

DAY 66

B.E.L.I.E.V.E

Become Excited Living In Encouragement,
Visualizing Everyday

DAY 67

R.E.A.D

Review Experiences As Delivered

"Seek wisdom, knowledge, and understanding and you will find them."

DAY 68

A.T.T.I.T.U.D.E

Awareness That Thinking Individuals Teach, Using Different Emotions

≈

DAY 69

P.A.S.S.I.O.N

Persistence Activating Strength Successfully In Our Nature

≈

DAY 70

W.I.S.D.O.M

Words Increase Success, Developing Our Minds

DAY 71

S.P.I.R.I.T

Source People Ignite, Retrieving Inner Toughness

≈

DAY 72

F.O.R.G.I.V.E

Freeing Our Reality Giving It Victory Eternally

≈

DAY 73

C.O.U.R.A.G.E

Creating Options Using Resilience And Great Effort

DAY 74

S.P.E.A.K

Show **P**eople **E**xcellence **A**nd **K**indness

"I encourage you to discover your purpose and do what you love to do."

DAY 75

T.H.A.N.K

Thoughtful **H**appy **A**ttitude **N**aturally **K**ept

DAY 76

G.O.D

Greatest **O**mniscient **D**eveloper

Mission

My life's mission is to develop leaders by giving them encouragement, and assisting them in discovering their self-worth. Simple Intelligence™ is the tool I use to help people think positively about their circumstances. I encourage you to discover your purpose and do what you love to do. My dream is to have Simple Intelligence™ be synonymous with common sense.

G.O.

"**G**et **O**ptimistic"

References

Alessandra, Dr. T., Retrieved from (http://www.youtube.com/watch?v=FrjpwXIwUuc&feature=related) 2011.

Buckingham, Marcus, Retrieved from (http://www.youtube.com/watch?v=wuZBJQAFOfM&feature=related) 2011.

Duplantis, Jessie, Retrieved from (http://www.youtube.com/watch?v=FlosLSf6RCA) 2011.

Ford, Henry, Retrieved from (http://www.goodreads.com/author/quotes/203714.Henry_Ford) 2011.

Rohn, Jim, Retrieved from (http://www.youtube.com/watch?v=YQ9_-DtLaNU) 2011.

Winfrey, Oprah, Retrieved from (http://www.oprah.com/own-master-class/Oprah-Winfreys-Master-Class-Quotes/5) 2011.

My Favorite Acronyms/Affirmations

Thanks again for reading and sharing *Simple Intelligence™* with your network. Visit **www.PierreCamp.com** daily for consistent leadership and personal development coaching. I look forward to hearing how *Simple Intelligence™* positively impacts your life. Email your testimonies to testimonies@pierrecamp.com.

PierreCamp
You are a Leader

17 Easy Ways to Use Your *"Simple Intelligence"* Acronyms

1. Place *Simple Intelligence* on your nightstand, so that you can study one or two acronyms every morning and night.
2. Read acronyms into a recorder and listen to yourself speaking positive words and affirmations.
3. Meditate on acronyms throughout your day to relax your mind.
4. Make acronyms your screensaver.
5. Make acronyms your cell phone background.
6. Read acronyms to your children to encourage their creative thought process.
7. Share acronyms in your blogs or daily emails.
8. Add an acronym to your email signature.
9. Share *Simple Intelligence* with a friend.
10. Use *Simple Intelligence* as a source that renews your mind.
11. Use *Simple Intelligence* as a memory exercise to increase your memory.
12. Use *Simple Intelligence* when you're unsure about challenging situations.
13. Record acronyms and use them as an alarm clock.
14. Use acronyms to inspire positive thinking.
15. Use acronyms to encourage others.
16. Put an acronym on your bathroom mirror.
17. Write an acronym on a small card, place it in your wallet and read it frequently throughout the day.

Simple Intelligence™ Leadership Model

Step 4: Getting Results

Step 3: Teamwork

Step 2: Building Relationships

Step 1: Personal Development

You are a leader

Copyright ©2012 Pierre Campbell
www.PierreCamp.com